# CELT
# SAINTS

# The Origins of Celtic Christianity

During the 'Dark Ages' of Europe, some remarkable men and women, fired by their new experience of Christianity, travelled from Ireland through Scotland and northern England, Wales and south-west Britain, sharing the light of Christ with all whom they met. Celtic 'saints', revered by the Church for their holiness and wisdom, took Christianity and literacy south through Brittany to southern Italy, east to the Ukraine, and north to the Faroes and Iceland. Monasteries and churches were founded wherever these Christian men and women travelled, teaching those they met of the love of God. The Celtic Church of the 5th and 6th centuries was not an identifiable organisation with a central leadership. Led by monastic abbots rather than diocesan bishops, it was marked out by its ethos, a philosophy markedly different from the Church of Rome.

No other Christian community has lived so closely with the Jewish Law. Each day and at every service passages of the Bible were read, the Psalms recited and the scriptures meditated upon. Those showing particular promise were entrusted with the careful copying of the Bible. Against the austerity and simplicity of their way of life, the elaborate and rich illuminations of their manuscripts show the central place the scriptures held. The Torah, the first five books of the Old Testament, were condensed for ease of use, and found great popularity among those who sought to explain the Bible to the illiterate.

The roots of Celtic monasticism are found in the lives of the Desert Fathers and Desert Mothers. During the 3rd century AD, Christians in Egypt fled the distractions and temptations of the cities to live solitary lives of prayer,

left:
Martin of Tours (316–397AD) who introduced monasticism to Europe, hoping it would bring Christian conversion and discipline to rural areas of Gaul.

right:
*Ninian's monastery at Whithorn became affectionately known as 'Candida Casa', or the White House, probably because its walls were painted with lime.*

above:
*The ruins of Whithorn Priory in Galloway, established by Ninian in about 397AD. Possibly the first stone church in Britain, it is certainly one of the oldest Christian centres in the British Isles.*

below:
*Ninian's Chapel, a 12th-century church marking the possible site of a Celtic hermitage on the Isle of Whithorn.*

meditation and fasting in the desert. Legends about St Anthony (251–356AD), his duels with the forces of evil, and years of solitude in the most inhospitable areas of the desert became the heroic model for others. However, some found the rigours of solitary life too hard, and chose to live in close proximity to their brethren, meeting on Saturdays and Sundays for services, but living apart through the week.

Celtic Christians called from the world to live as monks and nuns followed their forebears into their own 'deserts', desiring separate and radical lives of prayer.

The forerunner of the Celtic Church in the British Isles was **Ninian**. He was born of noble parents on the banks of the Solway Firth in about 360AD. As a young man he undertook a pilgrimage to Rome, where he was made a bishop by the Pope. On his way home, he is said to have visited **Martin of Tours**, and was impressed by the monastic principle of monks setting themselves apart to pray. Returning to Scotland, Ninian established a monastery and school at Whithorn in Galloway. Its fame spread rapidly, drawing people from all over the Celtic world; Patrick himself may have spent time in study there. A catechism supposedly written by Ninian claimed that the fruit of study was 'to perceive the eternal word of God reflected in every plant and insect, every bird and animal, and every man and woman'.

reland's patron saint, **Patrick**, was probably born in north-west Britain, son of a church deacon and grandson of a Christian priest. At the age of 16, he was taken captive by pirates and sold into slavery in Ireland, where he began to explore for himself the mysteries of the Christian faith. In his autobiography, one of the few pieces of Celtic writing where authorship is known, Patrick writes, 'I had to stay all night in the forests and on the mountains looking after the sheep, and I would wake to pray before dawn in all weathers; snow, frost and rain; I felt no fear, nor did I feel sleepy, because the Spirit of God was so fervent within me.'

After six years in slavery, God instructed Patrick in a dream to leave Ireland and return to his home. Escaping from his master, Patrick was guided some 200 miles to a ship which took him back to Britain. Eventually he returned to his home where he was trained and ordained as a priest. Patrick had a series of dreams which called on him to return once again to Ireland as a missionary and, against the wishes of his family, he made his way through Britain, possibly via Auxerre in Gaul, and on to Armagh in about 433AD.

There was already some missionary activity in Ireland, and Patrick worked tirelessly baptizing and confirming Christians, and ordaining those with education and a calling to the priesthood. Although not a monk himself, he encouraged men and women to embrace the monastic life and his deep love and pastoral care for the people of Ireland led him to travel through the land bringing the gospel to those who followed the ancient Druidic cults.

*below:*
*Through Patrick's zeal and the work of later saints such as Kevin, the church in Ireland was a beacon of light. Shown below is Kevin's church at Glendalough; it stands in a deep wooded valley between two lakes, ringed by the Wicklow hills.*

*left:*
*A Celtic high cross, intricately carved with knotwork and biblical scenes, marking the site of an important Christian event or symbolizing the protective power of the cross on which Christ died.*

left:
*The Gallarus Oratory on the Dingle peninsular, County Kerry, the best-preserved Celtic building in the British Isles, whose stone walls are corbelled, each course being of smaller stones than the layer beneath. Eventually they meet at the top to form a watertight roof.*

## PART OF 'ST PATRICK'S BREASTPLATE'

*At Tara today in this fateful hour
I place all heaven with its power
and the sun with its brightness
and the snow with its whiteness
and the fire with all the strength it has
and the lightning with its rapid wrath
and the winds with their swiftness
along their path
and the sea with its deepness
and the rocks with their steepness
and the earth with its starkness;
all these I place, by God's almighty help and grace,
between myself and the powers of darkness.*

Legend has it that Patrick lit a fire in celebration of Easter on the very night that Loegaire, High King of Ireland, was lighting his own fire to celebrate the rebirth of spring. Angered, the king called his Druid priests to him, and was further enraged when they prophesied that the fire Patrick had lit would burn forever, overcoming the king's own fire. Loegaire led an army forward from Tara, and as they challenged

Patrick, they saw him lift his arms in prayer before escaping into the night with his disciples. Further trials of strength ensued, but the God of Patrick always proved to be superior to that of the Druid priests. Eventually the High King allowed Patrick to preach Christianity in his realms, although he himself remained resolutely pagan.

Patrick is said to have taught the mystery of the Trinity using the shamrock as his illustration. On a single stem three separate leaves are joined to form a single whole, as God the Father, Son and Spirit are three that form a perfect whole. He is also credited with St Patrick's Breastplate, a hymn of protection probably belonging to the 8th century, epitomizing the *caim*. This was a traditional form of prayer which surrounded the person with an imaginary circle, not of magic but of the presence of God, and protected him from evil.

Patrick died near Wicklow, where his missionary journey began. Some traditions maintain that Patrick is buried at Downpatrick and many have claimed to possess his relics. Patrick's Roman training encouraged him to organize the Irish Church with powerful bishops enforcing moral and spiritual discipline. The Celtic Church preferred to embrace an ascetic tradition where monks and nuns taught the faith by example. But because of Patrick's zeal, the Irish Church became a beacon of light in an otherwise darkened Europe, and the Golden Age of the Saints had begun.

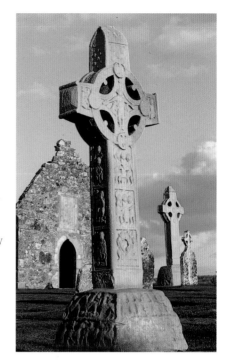

C eltic monastic settlements were usually established without there being any intention of founding a large community. A hermit built his cell in a place of solitude, a 'desert', and cleared an area of land on which to grow food. Gradually others would be drawn to join him, clearing more land and establishing their own cells nearby. Each monastery had huts set aside for travellers and the sick, for the principle of hospitality was important in the Celtic tradition. Finally a wooden chapel or oratory was constructed in which the community could meet to exercise the discipline of regular prayer. Some of these communities consisted of fewer than ten people while others might consist of hundreds or even thousands. The leader or abbot of the monastery was regarded as a wise spiritual director rather than a strict disciplinarian, although any bishops living within a monastery came under his authority.

Monks and nuns enjoyed a life of freedom compared with their continental Roman brethren, usually meeting together only once a day for worship and eucharist, and establishing their own patterns of prayer, work and study in their cells. Perseverance through recitation of the Psalms was at the centre of Celtic monastic prayer. All 150 Psalms were learnt by heart and it was usual to recite as

*right:*
*Tara, ancient capital of Ireland, where the remains include three different forts and a banqueting hall. The Druid priests of the High King challenged Patrick at Loegaire's fort and found Patrick's God to be more powerful than their own. Patrick is said to have prayed and the snow conjured up by the Druid priests melted away. A second prayer saved Patrick's youngest disciple from the fire into which the Druids had thrown him.*

many as 50 at one time. Fasting, silence and abstinence from sleep were practised regularly. Penitential positions of prayer were common – for example standing for long periods in cold water with arms outstretched. By subjugating their bodies, some Celtic Christians believed that their souls would be released and rise to God.

The Roman Church often claimed that Celtic Christianity was simply an extension of Celtic Druidism, the pre-Christian religion of the Celts. This accusation was mainly levelled at the British-born Pelagius, who argued with Augustine of Hippo, a theologian, about predestination. Unlike Augustine, who saw everything as pre-ordained by God, Pelagius argued that individuals also had moral responsibility for their own actions, because God had given them free will. Pelagius's recognition of the struggle between the grace of God and the will of His people was at the heart of Celtic Christianity. God's grace was to be seen in all aspects of the natural world, and the curtain between the material and spiritual worlds was thin.

Larger monasteries attracted pupils, often the children of royal households and landowners, who learnt to read and write, to sing and to appreciate the arts. They lived the full rigours of the religious life, taking part in manual labour as well as in daily prayer and study.

The Celtic Church was not afraid to assimilate with the culture in which it found itself, and art thrived and was refined in the monastic setting. The *Lindisfarne Gospels* and the *Book of Kells* reveal in their margins and painted pages small animals and mythical doodles, designs from pagan art now sanctified to the glory of God.

The wooden crosses set aside at places for preaching and at important memorial sites were gradually replaced by permanent standing crosses made of stone. The Latin-style cross was too tall to be surrounded by the circle of the much earlier Chi-Rho symbol, so a stylised circle simply embraced the shaft and crossing. Crosses at Clonmacnois in Ireland, Margam in Wales and Iona in Scotland, among many other high crosses to be found all over the Celtic world, are carved with Bible stories and intricate abstract designs testifying symbolically to the mystery of the faith.

**W**omen held a significant place in the Celtic Church, for the Celtic Christians had been influenced by the Druid religion that had gone before, and both men and women held authority in Celtic monasteries. Many communities were mixed, with monks and nuns living within conjoined enclosures, and some of those involved in monastic life were married; a female abbot was always called upon to oversee these double monasteries. The monastery at Kildare founded by **Brigid** was for a time the largest settlement in Ireland, renowned for its generous hospitality and fondly known as 'the City of the Poor'.

Legends about Brigid are exaggerated, not least because the Druid goddess of fertility was celebrated on the same feast day, and stories about the two have become linked. However, some have a ring of truth, and it seems that Brigid, having been baptized by Patrick himself, was determined to lead a religious life, against the wishes of her parents. Eventually her father is said to have taken her to the King of Leinster, hoping to sell her into slavery. As Brigid waited outside the castle, a leper came to beg for alms, and when her father returned, he found she had given away his sword. The king declared that Brigid's goodness was untamable, and that he was therefore unwilling to hinder her service to God.

Brigid was a born leader, and soon after establishing her cell at Kildare others joined her. With 12 disciples, she asked a travelling bishop, Mel, to pray for God's blessing on them as they took their vows as nuns. As the bishop lifted his arm in blessing he saw tongues of fire descending on Brigid's head, and the Holy Spirit caused him to speak over her the words of consecration of a bishop. Whatever the truth of this story, Brigid travelled widely, holding some form of authority within the Church which enabled her to preach to rich and poor alike, and to speak at Church synods. Legends about her hospitality abound, particularly regarding her cows, which were often milked three times a day to supply refreshment for unexpected guests. Great miracles of healing occurred, and Brigid was greatly loved for her faith, one bishop describing her as 'the Mary of the Gaels'.

The Celtic saint **Finnian** was born and educated in Leinster, later travelling to Wales to study in the monastic traditions of Cadoc and Illtud. Of the six monasteries he established, the largest was Clonard in County Meath, home, according to a later book of the saint's life, to 3,000 monks. **Ciaran**, a carpenter's son, studied at Clonard before his ordination on the Aran Islands. The monastery he established at Clonmacnois in 545AD became a centre for learning, sometimes described as Ireland's Celtic university. He died only months after establishing the community.

Educated by monks, **Kevin** chose to become a hermit. He is said to have attended Ciaran on his deathbed, but the rest of his life was spent at Glendalough where he built his cell. As disciples gathered around him, the Bronze Age barrow where he lived became too crowded, and the monastery moved further down the valley. Kevin withdrew to seek solitude by the upper lake, and he is often represented holding the nest of a blackbird, said to have laid her eggs in the palm of his hand while he was at prayer. The saint is reputed to have stayed in this position until the eggs hatched, illustrating the high regard the Celtic saints had for the natural world. Creation was seen as a mirror reflecting the glories of Heaven.

Irish monasticism flourished under these and many other saints, holy men and women burning with a zeal to serve God. With high ideals, they dedicated themselves to prayer and work; many gave hospitality to the poor and sick; some taught the faith that they themselves had learnt; others left their homes and monasteries to take the Kingdom of God beyond the Irish shores. Saints such as Piran sailed south towards Cornwall and Brittany, Brendan voyaged west into uncharted seas, and Columba went north-east to Scotland.

*left:*
*A page from the 'Book of Kells', probably written and illuminated on Iona and removed to Kells, site of Columba's most important monastery in Ireland, for safekeeping. It is now at Trinity College, Dublin.*

*far left:*
*One of the four evangelical symbols at the opening of St Mark's Gospel in the 'Book of Kells'.*

*above:*
*A page of the 'Stowe Missal', the oldest surviving prayer book of the Celtic Church.*

*left:*
*The 12th-century doorway of Clonfert Cathedral, a tiny church in a bleak and desolate area of peat bog in Galway, site of Brendan's monastery.*

# COLUMBA, DOVE OF THE CHURCH

**G**entle pastor, earnest scholar and rugged sailor, **Columba** was born and educated in Ireland. Until the age of about 40, Columba travelled throughout Ireland setting up monastic centres of learning and evangelism, including those at Kells and Derry. But in about 563 AD, he is alleged to have engaged in a dispute over the copyright of a manuscript which led to the slaughter of thousands of soldiers. Overwhelmed by remorse, Columba left Ireland determined to atone for his actions by winning as many souls for Christ as had been lost in battle. Legend records how he chose to live on Iona because from its shores he could not see his homeland.

The ordered way of life that Columba developed for the monastery on Iona became a model for other Celtic monasteries. It required that the monks lived only for God, praying constantly, offering hospitality to all, centring their conversations on God and the scriptures, owning no luxuries, eating only when hungry and sleeping only when tired. The monks shared in the heavy labour of the community, but some, the seniors, were also required to lead worship, study and copy the scriptures. Working brothers concentrated on farming and fishing, while novices

*right:*
The 13th-century Iona Abbey, a Benedictine monastery which replaced the wood and stone buildings of Columba's monastery founded in 563 AD.

*below left:*
The 'Cathach of Columba', oldest extant Irish manuscript of the Psalter and earliest example of Irish writing, over whose ownership Columba is said to have fought, leading to his self-imposed exile on Iona.

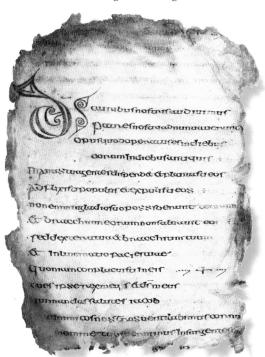

studied in preparation for taking their monastic vows. According to Bede, the chronicler of the Celtic Church in the 8th century, the Iona community was characterized by 'their purity of life, love of God and loyalty to the monastic rule'.

Legend has it that one day Columba saw a woman collecting nettles to make soup as her cow had not yet calved. Reflecting on this, he decided that he too would only eat nettle soup. 'If this woman eats nettles in expectation of a calf, how much more should I in expectation of Christ's kingdom.' The monk who prepared Columba's food was anxious for his beloved abbot's health, and supplemented the soup with milk. Columba thrived on his nettle soup and urged others in the monastery to partake with him. The monk whose task it was to prepare the soup was in a dilemma, for the milk quota was soon used up. When the monk confessed, Columba laughed: 'It is God's joke on me. It was only pride that led me to tell others of my diet, so I deserved to be tricked'.

As the community grew, so did its influence, and kings and princes sought Columba for his wise counsel. The sons of royalty and the nobility were sent to Iona for education in the scriptures and the arts. And Columba and his monks also travelled widely, spreading the Christian message and founding churches and monasteries. When Columba died in

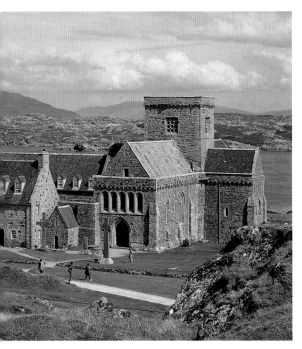

Columba's biographer said that in the week before his death Columba travelled about Iona, blessing and encouraging all whom he met. As he rested by the roadside, a favourite horse came and placed its head upon the old man's breast, sensing his imminent death. Columba's attendant came to drive the horse away, but Columba forbad him, saying 'You, a man of rational soul, can know nothing of my departure except what I tell you. This dumb creature, possessing no reason, has been told by the Creator Himself that I am about to leave'. Columba, in Gaelic 'Columcille', the Dove of the Church, is said to have died at the altar of his church, face radiant with joy, and hand outstretched in blessing.

597AD, he left a rich inheritance of peace previously unknown to the kingdoms in Scotland. Civil peace was not to last, however, for Iona, in common with other communities in Ireland, Northumbria and Scotland, was ravaged by Viking invaders. Gradually life on Iona became untenable, and most of the community returned to Ireland, taking their library with them.

left:
One of three high crosses, carved in the 8th century, standing in front of Iona Abbey.

right:
The chapel of St Oran in whose cemetery Columba is said to be buried with over 40 kings from Scotland, Ireland and England.

# ThE CALL TO NORThUMBRIA

C olumba's death in 597AD coincided with the arrival of Augustine in Canterbury. Britain now had two missionary movements, the Celtic Church from the north and the Roman Church from the south. Paulinus arrived in Northumbria from Kent in 625AD as companion to Ethelburga, Edwin's queen. When Edwin himself was converted to Christianity, thousands followed their king to be baptized. Cadwalla and pagan king Penda soon defeated Edwin and attempted to stamp out Christianity in Northumbria, but in 633AD **Oswald**, Edwin's nephew, returned to fight off the violence and injustices of Penda's reign.

The armies met on Hadrian's Wall at Heavenfield, near Hexham. Oswald set up a high wooden cross, and his army prayed beneath it for God's help. It is said that Oswald had a vision of Columba assuring him of victory, and the next day, despite being heavily outnumbered, Oswald won and established his residence at Bamburgh. He had been educated on Iona and, seeking to restore Christianity, sent to Iona for a missionary to carry the light of Christ to Northumbria. The first abortive mission was led by Corman who returned to Iona dismissive of this 'obstinate, barbarous people'. Hearing the report, the heart of one man, **Aidan**, was stirred with compassion for Northumbria, and he left his island home with 12 companions.

*right:*
The court of Oswald was built on the rocky crags at Bamburgh, where the castle now stands.

*below left:*
The statue of Aidan on Holy Island carries the flame of Christianity which spread throughout Northumbria and on into Europe.

*below:*
Lindisfarne Priory, the 11th-century Norman church built to re-establish a Christian community on Holy Island following the evacuation of the island after Viking raids in 875AD.

Aidan established a monastery on Holy Island, or Lindisfarne as it is also known. Looking across the sea to Oswald's court at Bamburgh, Aidan's monastic community was cut off twice each day by the tide, but joined to the mainland by a causeway as the tide receded. It was to become the cradle of Christianity in north-east England through succeeding generations, a place where nature, work and prayer interwove.

*right:*
*The interior of Cedd's church at Bradwell-on-Sea in Essex, established in about 654AD. The nave is all that remains of the church, which was built from the stone of an earlier Roman fort on the same site.*

distributed among the crowd. Aidan, moved by what he had seen, took the king's right hand and blessed it. Oswald was killed in battle in 642AD and his body was sacrificially mutilated by Penda. Bede records that Oswald's hand did not wither, being preserved by the blessing it had received. His head was also recovered and was later buried in Durham Cathedral beside Cuthbert.

Oswald opened Northumbria to the Christian faith, and this was continued by the kings who followed him. Oswin, one of the kings who followed Edwin, gave Aidan a horse from the royal stables to aid him in his travels. Aidan gave the horse to the first poor person he met, preferring to travel on foot like those with whom he was sharing the gospel. On his travels he would stop and speak to everybody, both rich and poor. If they were not Christians, he would invite them to embrace the mystery of faith and be baptized; if they were already believers he sought to strengthen their faith. When he died in 651AD, having spent 16 years in Northumbria, the fire of Christianity was burning bright in this area and beyond.

Aidan was supported by Oswald who accompanied him in his early travels, acting as translator and sharing the work of spreading Christianity. Oswald became renowned as a man of justice and compassion. One Easter, the poor came to beg for alms at the castle gate. Aidan was about to bless the feast when Oswald snatched up a large silver platter and had both food and pieces of the platter

Among those who were schooled in Christianity on Holy Island were two brothers, **Chad** and **Cedd**. The brothers were made bishops and Cedd was sent to Mercia where Peada, son of Penda, had been converted to Christianity and allowed monks from Holy Island to evangelize among his people. Cedd then became bishop to the Saxons in Anglia, where he established churches and monasteries; the tiny church at Bradwell-on-Sea in Essex remains as a testimony to his work. His brother Chad was sent to Ireland to study, and on his return became bishop of Mercia, establishing his episcopal centre at Lichfield, whose cathedral bears his name. Like Aidan, he travelled widely on foot, miracles accompanying his proclamation of the gospel.

While tending sheep in the Scottish borders, the young **Cuthbert** saw a vision of a great light in the sky and angels carrying a holy soul to heaven. He immediately left the fields to offer himself for the religious life at nearby Melrose monastery. There he learnt of the death of Aidan, and vowed to continue Aidan's work in spreading the gospel throughout Northumbria.

Cuthbert sought a life of solitude but was frequently called out of his cell for the sake of his monasteries and to preach widely. Wherever he spoke, crowds flocked to hear him and miracles were recorded. Feeling hungry one day, Cuthbert prayed and an eagle is said to have brought a salmon to his feet. Cutting the fish in two, Cuthbert returned half the fish to the bird, while he and his companions shared the other half.

In 661AD Cuthbert became prior of Holy Island, and he often withdrew to a small rocky outcrop which is now known as Cuthbert's Island. Later he withdrew further into solitude, building a cell and oratory on the Inner Farne. This island had no water, no food and no trees. A well was carved from the rock, and seed was sown in shallow soil, often to be washed away by storms and tides. Cuthbert's life of solitude was broken by visitors seeking counsel from this wise man, but when he was alone he would undertake harsh penances, standing all night waist deep in the sea. Legends say that sea otters dried his feet in the morning, warming his frozen legs.

After ten years on the Inner Farne, Cuthbert was persuaded to return to Holy Island as bishop, but two years later he withdrew into solitude again, dying shortly afterwards. His body was buried on Holy Island. The first Viking raid on the English coast was directed at Holy Island in 793AD, and the monks moved Cuthbert's body inland, fearing for its safety. Eventually, the coffin was moved to Durham, where in 995AD a church was built, and later Cuthbert's remains were laid behind the altar of the great Norman cathedral.

*above centre:*
Cuthbert's pectoral cross made from Northumbrian gold and inlaid with garnets, taken from his tomb in Durham Cathedral in 1827.

*above:*
St Cuthbert is entreated to accept the bishopric of Lindisfarne; this illustration is from a 12th-century manuscript.

## THE VENERABLE BEDE

The 7th-century chapel of Bede's monastery remains as the chancel of St Paul's, Jarrow. **Bede** entered the monastery school at Monkwearmouth as a child in 680AD, and spent most of his life working a few miles away at Jarrow. The monastery there boasted a magnificent library endowed by Benedict Biscop, a nobleman serving in the court of King Oswy who later, as a monk, established this monastery. Bede devoted his life to writing church history, using as his sources the numerous learned and well-travelled scholars who visited Jarrow. From 'The Ecclesiastical History of the English People' we have learned more about Christianity in Northumbria and beyond than from any other source. Legend has it that when the stonemason was carving an inscription on Bede's tomb, he was unable to think of an appropriate adjective to describe such an important man. When he returned to the tomb the next morning, the mason found 'Venerable', meaning worthy of honour, inscribed there, as though carved by an angel of God.

*below:*
The tomb of the Venerable Bede, chronicler of the Church, in the Galilee Chapel of Durham Cathedral.

# HILDA OF WHITBY

orn of noble parents in 614AD, **Hilda** was baptized by Paulinus, and remained true to her faith through the dark reign of Penda and Cadwalla. When Aidan came to Northumbria and began to convert people to Christianity, Hilda decided to set aside her royal heritage and become a nun. She planned to join a community in Gaul, but Aidan called her to return to Northumbria, where she lived first beside the river Wear and later as abbot at the monastery at Hartlepool. There she developed a Rule, a way of living which brought discipline and order to the daily life of the community. Composite Rules, based on the monastic influences of the abbot, allowed for a measure of flexibility in the running of each monastery.

Hilda was made abbot of Whitby in 657AD, creating there a double monastery housing both monks and nuns. Under her leadership, Whitby became a centre for learning where literature and the arts were encouraged and she became patron to the uneducated Caedmon, a gifted poet and lay brother whose songs and stories helped illiterate Christians to understand the scriptures.

The Synod of Whitby hosted by Hilda in 664AD brought to a head the struggles between the Roman insistence on absolute authority and conformity, and the Celtic desire for continuing autonomy and mutual respect. Colman, abbot of Holy Island, Cedd and Hilda could not prevent the persuasive and politically astute Wilfrid, abbot of Ripon and supporter of the Roman tradition, from eloquently swaying the Synod in favour of Rome. In the eyes of the ecclesiastical court, the monastic traditions of Ireland, Iona and Northumbria were crushed. Celtic monasteries in England were overtaken by the authoritarian disciplines of the Roman Church; conformity and ritual replaced spontaneity, and abstract piety overshadowed the ordinary.

*Hilda developed a centre of learning for priests and lay people on the cliffs above Whitby. Her monastery was destroyed by the Vikings in 867AD and the ruins of a later medieval abbey stand on the site.*

I n Wales and south-west Britain, Christian men and women established hermitages and monasteries in the Celtic tradition. The father of the Celtic saints in Wales was **Dyfrig**, probably the first bishop of south-west Wales and abbot on Caldey Island. Biographers of the period suggest that he was a disciple of St Germanus of Auxerre at the monastery founded by Cassian near Marseilles. **Illtud** may also have followed St Germanus, and founded his monastery at Llantwit Major, Vale of Glamorgan, where many came to study the scriptures, philosophy, poetry, art, rhetoric and arithmetic.

The monastery grew in reputation and size, and ran out of arable land. There is a legend that Illtud used his staff to mark out a furrow at the low watermark, which he forbad the sea to pass. The sea did not transgress his command, and the reclaimed land provided amply for the monastery and its guests. Illtud often withdrew to a place of solitude for prayer, probably an oratory at Oxwich, although he also travelled widely, making pilgrimages to St Michael's Mount and to Brittany, where he is remembered at Dol as 'the most learned of all the Britons'.

David's mother Non is reputed to have been a holy woman of noble birth, possibly a nun, suggesting that not all those called to a religious life were also called to celibacy. **David**, patron saint of Wales, built his first monastery near his birthplace, a collection of wooden buildings which were replaced by St David's Cathedral in the 12th century. Monks associated with monasteries founded by David lived in strict

*left:*
*The Ogham stone on Caldey Island inscribed in this ancient burial language and in Latin, bidding those who pass to pray for Cadoc, the monk reputed to have admitted Illtud to the monastic life.*

austerity, combining heavy manual labour, fervent prayer, and a sparse diet of bread, water and vegetables, mainly wild leeks, which have since become the national emblem of Wales.

At Llanddewi Brevi, near Tregaron, David conducted his most famous mission. It is said that, as he preached, a mound grew under his feet, enabling him to be seen and heard by the huge crowds which had gathered. In order to restore order after the great pestilence of 547AD, David spoke again at Llanddewi Brevi to the assembled Welsh Church, and was

*above:*
David is thought to have founded
a monastery on the site of
St David's Cathedral in the 6th
century, hence its Welsh name
'Tyddewi', David's house.

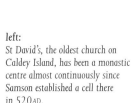

*left:*
St David's, the oldest church on
Caldey Island, has been a monastic
centre almost continuously since
Samson established a cell there
in 520AD.

proclaimed archbishop. David travelled widely, to Bath, Coldingham and to Glastonbury, fabled as the last resting place of the Holy Grail, said to have been brought to Britain by Joseph of Arimathea.

**Samson** joined the monastery at Llantwit Major as a child, and was educated and then ordained as deacon and priest. He went to live with Dyfrig on Caldey Island where he met Irish missionaries returning from Rome. He travelled to Ireland with them, where he acquired a chariot, in which he is

*above:*
The chapel and well marking the
birthplace of David near St David's
Cathedral, and dedicated to Non,
a holy woman of noble birth and
mother of David.

*left:*
The Tor at Glastonbury in
Somerset. The tor and the abbey
have long been claimed by
Christians as a site of pilgrimage
and hermitage. It was here that
David is said to have established
a church and where his remains
were later venerated.

said to have carried his books throughout his lifetime. He did not return to Caldey Island for long but set out once more, first to Cornwall and thence from Golant, near Fowey, to Dol in Brittany. Legend has it that Samson converted one pagan tribe by using an iron bar to carve a cross upon a granite Ogham stone inscribed with ancient symbols. Ogham stones marked a holy place, a memorial or a grave.

Much of our knowledge of 6th-century life comes from the writings of **Gildas**, a Northumbrian born in 500AD, and educated by Illtud. Gildas withdrew into solitude to write his diatribe on the laxity and corruption of the Church, *The Ruin of Britain*. Gildas wrote in Latin and used it to communicate with other Celtic peoples whose everyday language differed from his own. In between his travels, he lived in a hermitage at Street, near Glastonbury, and he died in Brittany in 570AD.

**Paul Aurelian**, also known as 'Paulinus' in parts of Wales, was educated at Llantwit Major, but left at the age of 16 to live as a hermit in Llandovery. As more disciples joined him he founded a monastery at Llanddeusant, on the inhospitable moorlands below the Black Mountain.

**A**s a 'journeyer for the love of Christ', Paul Aurelian left Wales when Mark, the Christian king of Cornwall, asked him to teach the people of Cornwall about Christ. Landing at Padstow, he travelled across Cornwall with his disciples. It is also likely that he visited his sister Sitofolla, who lived in a monastery near St Michael's Mount. From Cornwall, Paul travelled on to Brittany where he was consecrated bishop of Leon, and St Pol de Leon became the first town in the new bishopric of Lower Brittany.

Some Celtic Christians travelled around the Celtic kingdoms of the British Isles and on into Europe, while others journeyed to places where Christianity had not yet been established. Their wanderings led to a separation from all they held dear, many pilgrims travelling for years and never returning to their homes. They were called by God to follow the example of Abraham, Paul of Tarsus and Columba, symbolized by the wild goose, a Celtic image of the Holy Spirit.

Some saints looked for remote sites, places without the distraction of the world, their motivation ascetic rather than evangelistic. Skellig Michael, a sharp peak of rock standing in the ocean off County Kerry, shows the degree of isolation and hardship the Celtic Christians were willing to accept. Monks built a monastery of six beehive huts and two oratories on a

### A CELTIC PILGRIMAGE TO CORNWALL

The patron saint of Cornwall, **Petroc**, is said to have come from South Wales some time in the 6th century. He lived for many years at Padstow, where the monastery he founded became the centre of his missionary activities. Later Petroc moved to Little Petherick where a mill and chapel were established, and he then withdrew into further solitude to a beehive cell on Bodmin Moor. **Neot** from Glastonbury also sought isolation there in the 9th century but was later joined by others and a monastery was founded. Other Cornish saints chose isolated sites on the edge of the sea. **Piran's** cell near Perranzabulo is now buried under sand dunes, and the church dedicated to Enodoc was disappearing but has been recovered from the encroaching sands. Lundy Island has a church dedicated to Endellion, where she is presumed to have spent time before joining the monastery at Tintagel.

bare ledge 600 feet (130m) above the sea, bringing earth and stone for building from the mainland. Those living on the Skellig survived on a diet of fish, sea birds and herbs, collecting rainwater in wells carved from solid rock. Like Lindisfarne and Iona, this island settlement was home for a wandering people in search of a clearer vision of God.

**Columbanus** is recognized as one of Ireland's greatest apostles because of his pioneering journey

**right:**
Beehive huts, part of an almost complete Celtic monastery including oratories and graveyard, surviving on Skellig Michael, 8 miles (11.6km) off the County Kerry coast.

**Brendan the Navigator**, founder of the monastery at Clonfert, grew up on the Dingle Peninsular. He started his journeying from the hills above Bantry Bay in County Cork. With 14 companions he built a boat of wood and hide and set off to find new lands. From Ireland via the monastery at Iona, Brendan and his companions are said to have travelled through the Faroes to Iceland, and on to Greenland and Newfoundland. His 'Journey of Life' was not only the voyage of a navigator, but a spiritual journey, for within the adventure of exploration was the on-going discovery of the scriptures and of the cycle of prayer central to monastic life. Biographies of Brendan may or may not be allegorical, but they illustrate the daring and astonishingly far-reaching travels of the Celtic saints.

through Europe. He was born in about 543AD, educated under Abbot Comgall at Bangor in Northern Ireland, and at the age of 57 began his 'voluntary exile for Christ'. With 12 companions, he established his first church in the Vosges in Gaul on the site of a temple to the goddess Diana, thereby consecrating a pagan site to the glory of God. After 13 years of travel, almost constantly at odds with the Roman Church for his Celtic Christian practices, Columbanus settled at Bobbio in the Apennines, where he died.

*above:*
*An illustration of Brendan the Navigator on his journey across the northern Atlantic in a coracle. From a manuscript in Heidelberg University Library.*

*right:*
*A Celtic cross on Bodmin Moor, one of many such crosses erected around the British Isles either to mark out meeting places for preaching and prayer or as memorials.*

*left:*
*Neot's well on Bodmin Moor, where the saint recited the Psalms daily and was said to have been rewarded with a miraculous and endless supply of fish.*

# CELTIC INHERITANCE

The Synod of Whitby in 664AD isolated Northumbria from its historical and spiritual roots in Iona and Ireland. Power became concentrated under Wilfrid in York. Gradually political alliances with southern kingdoms of England brought closer links with the bishopric at Canterbury, and Celtic spirituality in Northumbria was replaced by Roman Church structures and rituals. But it was Viking raids on monastic settlements which brought confusion and dispersal to the wider Celtic Church in the British Isles.

Viking raiders were drawn to the riches the monasteries held without any form of defence. After the first attack on Northumbria in 793AD, there followed raids on Iona and island communities in Ireland. Monks who were not killed were taken captive, and so many fled inland taking books and relics with them. After a lull of some 30 years, the Vikings returned, intent on permanent conquest. These were years of fear and uncertainty. Many saw the Vikings as a sign of God's displeasure for their spiritual laxity; not everyone could live the life of prayer demanded by the Celtic saints.

In Ireland, groups of monks calling themselves *culdees*, companions of God, clung to Celtic monasticism, and inland monasteries continued to flourish. Stone-carvers on Anglesey and in Glamorgan continued to work using Celtic designs, and Cornish Christianity remained constant to Celtic forms of prayer until the 12th century. But gradually even Wales, Cornwall and Ireland were absorbed by the Roman Church. Some monasteries continued to function, Iona becoming a Benedictine abbey and Holy Island serving as a priory under the Benedictine order in Durham.

Even as late as the 14th century, groups of Celtic monks could be found in the Scottish Highlands and islands. In the 19th century a Scottish clergyman, Alexander Carmichael, travelled widely in these areas. He discovered an oral tradition of prayer handed down through the generations which bore a striking resemblance to prayers found in the early Celtic Church. Although Christian spirituality had been adulterated by pagan imagery, his collected writings, the *Carmina Gadelica*, bear witness to the spirituality of a vanished age.

We follow our Celtic inheritance through pilgrimage, seeking places that have lain dormant for centuries. The Celtic saints were tireless in their worship of God, and in the ancient, broken stones of their buildings and crosses a strange beauty is found. The spiritual realities that the Celtic saints knew are increasingly relevant in the confusion of the 20th century. Old treasures, both temporal and spiritual, are being rediscovered, touching the hearts of many who are asking 'Where is the good way? Ask for the old paths, and you will find rest for your souls' (Jeremiah 6:16).

*Some modern-day pilgrims ascending Croagh Patrick in County Mayo. Patrick is said to have fasted here for 40 days in prayer and penitence, seeking guidance from God.*